PAUL McCARTNEY

Ecce Cor Meum

Behold My Heart

FOR SOPRANO SOLO, BOY TREBLES, CHORUS AND ORCHESTRA

FABER *ff* MUSIC

IN ASSOCIATION WITH MPL COMMUNICATIONS

Ecce Cor Meum is recorded by the same forces as in the world premiere
on EMI Classics – (CD 0946 3 70424 2 7)

To buy Faber Music publications or to find out about the full range of titles available
please contact your local music retailer or Faber Music sales enquiries:

Faber Music Limited, Burnt Mill, Elizabeth Way, Harlow, CM20 2HX England
Tel: +44 (0)1279 82 89 82   Fax: +44 (0)1279 82 89 83
sales@fabermusic.com   fabermusic.com

The world premiere performance was given by Kate Royal (soprano),
with the Academy of St Martin in the Fields, London Voices,
the Boys of Magdalen College Choir, Oxford and King's College Choir, Cambridge,
conducted by Gavin Greenaway, in the Royal Albert Hall, London, on 3 November 2006

The U.S. premiere performance was given by Kate Royal (soprano),
with the Orchestra of St Luke's, the Concert Chorale of New York, and The American Boychoir,
conducted by Gavin Greenaway, in Carnegie Hall, New York City, on 14 November 2006

Duration: 57 minutes

Orchestra

2 Flutes
2 Oboes
2 Clarinets in B♭
2 Bassoons

2 Horns in F
2 Trumpets in B♭
(optionally doubling Piccolo trumpets)

Timpani

Percussion
Side drum

Harp
Organ

Strings

Full score and orchestral parts available on hire
from Faber Music

Contents

ECCE COR MEUM

Behold My Heart

I – SPIRITUS

Words and Music by
Paul McCartney

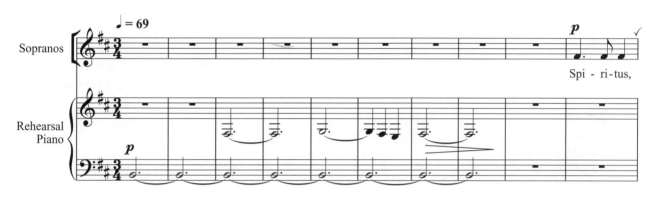

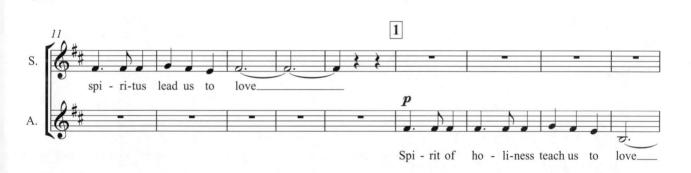

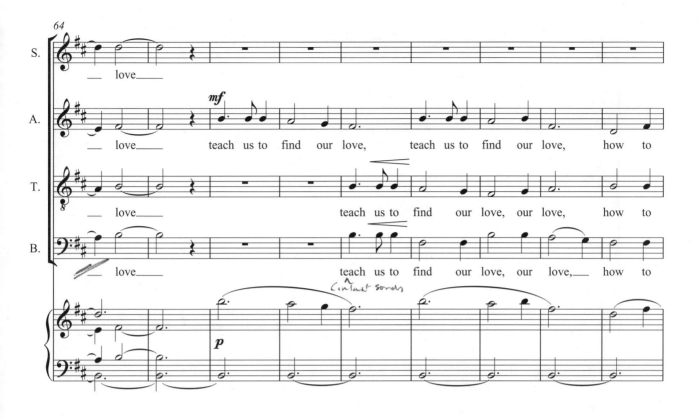

4

6

14

where would we hide, where could we run to hide.

Show us how to find our-selves

Show us how to find our-selves

guide us from a - bove,

guide us from a - bove   teach us

our   love   our   love   love

our   love   our   love   love

II – GRATIA

hold so dear this hum-ble state of grace In the night a

prize for this we hold so dear ah

prize hold dear state of grace ah

prize and hold dear state of grace ah

daf-fo-dil is bat-tered by the fa-ther of all storms. Day-break sees it

daf-fo-dil bat-tered by the fa-ther of all storms. Day-break sees it

prize and this we hold so dear this hum-ble state of grace ah

ah ah ah

INTERLUDE

S. hold so dear this hum-ble state of grace_____

A. hold dear this hum-ble state of grace_____

T. hold this hum-ble state of grace_____

B. hold this hum-ble state of grace_____

A. ah ah_____ ah ah

T. ah ah_____ ah_____

B. ah ah_____ ah_____

46

III – MUSICA

52

help to re-veal my in - ner light.

help to re-veal my in - ner light.

help to re-veal my light.

breath ber. diminuendo

help to re-veal my in - ner light.

In - ner

In - ner

In - ner

56

When I feel real joy flow-ing deep and warm, still it brings a spe - cial glow, to this heart of mine for it means__ so__ much more than you will ev - er know_____

When I feel real joy flow-ing deep and warm, still it brings a spe-cial glow, to this

trea - sure of my soul

I can feel real joy so deep and warm still it brings a spe-cial glow_____ to this

62

Tr. love

mu-sic is the trea-sure that we all can

S. we all seek the plea-sures of love

A. we all seek the plea-sures of love

Tr. bring

S. we are hap-py if we smile but are de-light-ed when we sing

A. we are hap-py if we smile but are de-light-ed when we sing

IV – ECCE COR MEUM

no - thing else re - mains.

no - thing else, no - thing else re - mains.

no - thing else, no - thing else re - mains.

no - thing else re - mains.

83

With - out truth false shades

With - out truth false shades

With - out truth false shades

With - out truth false shades

118